MW01131330

Stoicism

for Kids

50 Original Stories to Discover the Power of Resilience, Wisdom, and Emotional Balance

Coordinator: Juan Rodriguez

Writers: Juan Rodriguez, Morgan Barrett, Anne Moore, Kavya Sharma

Illustrators: Mary Banks, Aryan Patel, Ming-Hui Zhang

Table of Contents

Become an Emotional Superhero!

With the exciting stories in this book, you'll discover the secrets of emotional control and unlock your full potential. From the fiery flames of anger to the icy chills of fear, you'll learn how to tame your emotions and use them to your advantage. This book will give you the tools you need to stay calm, cool, and collected.

So if you want to learn how to stay in control and conquer your emotions like a superhero, check out "Emotional Control for Kids"!

Introduction

Have you ever felt angry, sad, or scared and didn't know what to do? Maybe you wanted to scream or cry, but you didn't feel like it would help. Well, there's a group of people called Stoics who knew just what to do in those situations!

Stoicism is an ancient philosophy that teaches us how to be strong, brave, and wise in difficult times. The Stoics were people who lived a long time ago, like the emperor Marcus Aurelius and the famous philosophers Epictetus and Seneca. They believed that we can't always control what happens to us, but we can control how we react to it.

Marcus Aurelius   Epictetus   Seneca

Stoicism is so good for people today because it teaches us how to be happy, even when things are tough. It teaches us how to be honest, humble, and kind. It teaches us how to be in control of our emotions and actions, and it teaches us how to be brave and strong, even when we're scared.

So come on a journey with us and discover the amazing world of Stoicism! You'll learn how to be kind, brave, and wise in any situation. You'll learn how to be happy, even when things are tough. And you'll learn how to be in control of your emotions and actions. It's time to become a Stoic!

Resilience and Perseverance

Explanation

Resilience and perseverance are like being a brave adventurer who doesn't give up, even when things get tough. Imagine you're climbing a mountain, and it's really hard. Maybe you're tired, hungry, or scared. But if you keep going, step by step, you'll get to the top and feel amazing!

Stoics believe that being resilient and perseverant helps you overcome challenges and achieve your goals. When you face a problem or a difficult situation, you can either give up or keep going. With resilience and perseverance, you keep going, even when it's hard.

When you're resilient and perseverant, you're also more confident and brave. Maybe you're trying something new, and you're not sure if you can do it. But if you keep trying and don't give up, you'll feel proud of yourself and be able to do more things in the future.

So be like a brave adventurer and use your resilience and

perseverance to climb your own mountains! It might be hard, but if you keep going and believe in yourself, you can overcome anything and achieve your dreams.

~ Zephyr and the Tornado ~

A Story About Resilience and Perseverance

Once upon a time, in a small town nestled in the heart of America, a powerful tornado touched down. The winds roared, the trees bent, and the houses shook. But one family was ready. They had prepared for this moment and rushed to the safety of their basement, huddling together as the tornado raged outside.

When the storm had passed, they emerged to find their home in ruins. The parents were devastated, but their son, a spunky and resilient boy named Zephyr, remained surprisingly upbeat. His parents were puzzled and asked him how he could be so positive in the face of such destruction.

Zephyr smiled and replied, "We're all safe, that's what matters. We can rebuild our home slowly, at our own pace. It'll take time, but we'll make it happen."

His parents were amazed by his stoic outlook and grateful for his wise words. Zephyr's resilience and positivity gave them the strength to pick up the pieces and start anew.

They took it one step at a time, rebuilding their home and their lives, with Zephyr leading the charge.

In the end, they emerged stronger and more united than ever before, thanks to the unwavering resilience of their young son, Zephyr.

~ The Student Who Never Gave Up ~

Once upon a time, there was a diligent student named Martin who had a passion for mathematics, but he always struggled with understanding complex equations. No matter how many hours he dedicated to studying, the numbers seemed to blur together, leaving him frustrated and disheartened.

Undeterred by the challenges, Martin made a firm decision not to surrender. He approached his teachers and sought their guidance, and they introduced him to exceptional tutors specialized in advanced mathematics. These tutors possessed a unique ability to break down complex concepts into simpler, relatable terms that finally made sense to Martin.

Though the journey wasn't without its hurdles, Martin persisted with unwavering determination. He spent countless nights poring over textbooks, seeking additional help, and practicing tirelessly until the solutions to those intricate equations revealed themselves before his eyes.

In a moment of courage, he decided to participate in a school math contest. To his astonishment, Martin emerged as the victor, defying all expectations. His triumph not only showcased his mathematical prowess but also served as a testament to his unwavering resilience.

Through his incredible journey of perseverance and resilience, Martin realized that hard work and determination could lead to remarkable achievements. Winning the math contest became a symbol of his unwavering spirit, showing him that with resilience, anything is possible. From that day forward, Martin continued to embrace challenges with confidence, knowing that his dreams were within reach if he never gave up.

~ The Persistent Penguins ~

Once upon a time in the frosty Antarctic, there lived two plucky penguin siblings named Polly and Peter. They spent their days waddling, sliding, and splashing in the icy waters with their friends.

One day, a challenging task arose: learning to catch fish for their family. Polly eagerly dove into the water, her beak snapping at the slippery fish. She missed many times, but her determination never wavered. With each attempt, she grew swifter and more skillful.

Peter, on the other hand, grew grumpy and impatient. He often quit, leaving the water with empty flippers. "I just can't do it!" he would exclaim, his little penguin brow furrowed in frustration.

One chilly evening, a fierce storm swept through their icy home, leaving the penguins with little food. Polly's fishing prowess kept her family fed, while Peter's lack of skills left him hungry and weak.

Seeing her brother struggle, Polly waddled over, her eyes

full of kindness. "Peter," she said, "I know it's tough, but we must keep trying. Remember, practice makes perfect!"

Peter sighed, his spirits lifted by Polly's encouraging words. Together, they braved the icy waters, their beaks snapping and diving until Peter finally caught his first fish!

From that day on, Peter learned the value of resilience and perseverance, and the penguin siblings became the most skillful fishers in their frosty Antarctic home.

~ The Explorer Who Found the Treasure ~

Once upon a time, there was a young adventurer named Ziggy, who set out to explore a dangerous jungle in search of a hidden treasure. Ziggy knew the journey wouldn't be easy, with rough terrain, hostile wildlife, and treacherous weather to contend with. But he was determined to succeed, and with his backpack full of supplies, he set off into the unknown.

As Ziggy ventured deeper into the jungle, he encountered all sorts of obstacles. There were steep cliffs to climb, raging rivers to cross, and thick vines to hack through. And everywhere he went, there seemed to be creatures lurking in the shadows, ready to pounce at any moment.

Ziggy persisted, refusing to give up despite the challenges. But when he finally reached the spot on the map where the treasure was supposed to be, he found nothing.

14

Ziggy searched high and low, digging and digging, but he couldn't find a single piece of treasure. He started to feel discouraged and almost gave up hope.

But then something amazing happened. Ziggy looked up and saw a breathtaking sunset from the top of the hill where he stood. The golden rays of the sun made everything shine and sparkle, creating a magnificent landscape. It was then that Ziggy realized that he had discovered the greatest treasure of all – perseverance!

With a renewed sense of purpose, Ziggy continued his journey back home, feeling proud of his determination to never give up. He knew that the adventure had been worth it, even without the treasure. For Ziggy had discovered that sometimes the greatest reward comes not from finding riches, but from persevering through adversity.

~ The Ant and the Sugar Cube ~

Once upon a time, in a bustling ant colony, there lived a little ant named Archie. One day, while out foraging for food, Archie stumbled upon a giant sugar cube! The sugar cube was so big that Archie knew he couldn't carry it back to the colony on his own.

But did Archie give up? No way! With a determined look in his little ant eyes, Archie began to chip away at the sugar cube, bit by bit. He worked tirelessly, day and night, never giving up on his quest for the sugary treasure.

The other ants in the colony watched in awe as Archie chipped away at the massive sugar cube. Some laughed and shook their heads, thinking he was crazy for even trying. But Archie kept at it, never losing faith in himself.

Finally, after what seemed like forever, Archie had chipped the sugar cube down to a manageable size. He picked up the tasty treat and made his way back to the colony, where he was greeted with cheers and applause.

The other ants crowded around, eagerly gobbling up the sweet sugar cube that Archie had worked so hard to bring back. And from that day forward, Archie was known as the little ant who never gave up.

~ Sammy's Inspiring Tale of Growth ~

A Story About Resilience and Perseverance

Once upon a time, there was a small seed named Sammy. Sammy was blown away from his parent plant and found himself in a patch of dry, cracked soil. The sun was hot,

and the wind was fierce. It was not the ideal place for a seed to grow. But Sammy was determined to make the best of it.

With a tiny green shoot, Sammy pushed through the hard soil. It was tough going, but Sammy refused to give up. Day by day, the shoot grew longer and stronger, reaching toward the sky. Even when it rained, the water barely reached Sammy, but still, he persevered.

The sun beat down relentlessly, and the wind never stopped blowing, but Sammy kept growing. Slowly but surely, he grew taller and stronger until one day, he blossomed into a beautiful plant. His leaves swayed in the breeze, and his flowers attracted bees and butterflies.

Sammy had proven that even in the toughest circumstances, with resilience and perseverance, anything is possible. And so, he continued to grow and thrive, inspiring other seeds to never give up on their dreams.

Courage

Courage is like being a knight who is not afraid to do what is right, even when it's scary or hard. Imagine you see someone being bullied, and you know it's wrong. If you have courage, you'll stand up for them, even if it means going against the bully.

Stoics believe that having courage helps you be a good person and make the world a better place. When you have courage, you can do things that are important, even if they're scary or hard. Maybe you have to give a speech in front of a lot of people, or you have to tell the truth even if it might get you in trouble. With courage, you can do these things and feel proud of yourself.

When you have courage, you're also more confident and respected. Maybe someone tries to pressure you to do something you know is wrong. If you have courage, you can say no and stand up for what you believe in. This helps you be a better friend and make better choices.

So be like a brave knight and use your courage to stand up for what is right and do things that are important, even when they're scary or hard. It might not always be easy, but with courage, you can make a big difference in the world.

~ Fiona's First Steps on Stage ~

Fiona was a shy little girl who loved to dance. She would twirl and spin in her room, her heart filled with joy. But the thought of dancing in front of others made her tummy churn with fear.

One day, her school announced a dance performance, and Fiona's friends excitedly signed up. They tried to persuade Fiona to join, but she hesitated. "What if I trip and fall? What if everyone laughs at me?" she worried.

The day of the performance arrived. Fiona watched from the sidelines as her friends leaped and swayed on stage, their faces beaming with happiness. The audience clapped and cheered, and Fiona felt a little tug in her heart.

Suddenly, her friend Lily noticed her and waved, motioning for her to join them on stage. Fiona's heart raced, and her palms grew sweaty. But she took a deep breath, mustered her courage, and stepped onto the stage.

As the music played, Fiona started to dance. Her fear melted away with each step, and she felt as light as a feather. Her friends danced around her, their eyes sparkling with joy.

Fiona twirled, jumped, and laughed, her heart swelling with pride. She realized that courage had given her the chance to share her love of dance with others, and she shined brighter than ever before.

~ The Bravest Bunny ~

Once upon a time, in a forest filled with tall trees and colorful flowers, there lived a bunny named Benny. Benny was a timid little bunny who loved to nibble on carrots and hop around with his bunny friends. But Benny had a secret – he was afraid of almost everything.

One day, a group of bullies came into the forest and started causing trouble. They pushed around the smaller animals and scared them with their loud voices. Benny's friends were too scared to do anything, but Benny knew he had to be brave.

He hopped over to the bullies and stood up tall on his hind legs. "Stop it!" he said. "Leave my friends alone!"

The bullies laughed and sneered. "What are you going to do, little bunny? You're too small to stop us!"

But Benny wasn't afraid anymore. He puffed up his chest and took a deep breath. Then he let out the loudest, fiercest bunny roar the forest had ever heard!

The bullies were so surprised that they stumbled backward

and tripped over each other. Benny's friends cheered and hugged him tightly.

From that day on, Benny was known as the bravest bunny in the forest. He still nibbled on carrots and hopped around with his friends, but now he did it with a little extra bounce in his step.

~ Lenny the Lion's Leap of Faith ~

In the heart of the jungle, Lenny the Lion was known for being a bit of a scaredy-cat. One sunny afternoon, his friends invited him on an adventure to explore the other side of a small ravine.

As they approached the ravine, Lenny's friends leaped across with ease. But Lenny hesitated, his heart pounding in his chest. "What if I don't make it? What if I fall?" he worried.

His friends cheered him on from the other side, but Lenny couldn't find the courage to jump. Disappointed, he watched them disappear into the lush greenery, their laughter echoing through the trees.

Later that day, Lenny's friends returned, their eyes wide with excitement. They shared tales of a hidden valley with a sparkling waterfall and the most beautiful flowers they'd ever seen.

Lenny's heart ached with longing. He knew he couldn't let

fear hold him back any longer. Taking a deep breath, he returned to the ravine and stared across the gap.

This time, with a burst of courage, Lenny leaped with all his might. He soared through the air and landed safely on the other side. His friends greeted him with hugs and cheers, proud of his bravery.

Together, they explored the enchanting valley, and Lenny discovered that with courage, he could conquer his fears and embrace life's greatest adventures.

~ The Little Bird with Big Courage ~

Once upon a time, in a lush green forest, lived a little bird named Pip. Pip was very small and had never flown before. He was afraid of heights and the idea of soaring up high in the sky terrified him. Pip's mother would try to teach him how to fly, but he always chickened out.

One day, Pip's mother was captured by a wicked owl. Pip knew he had to do something to save her. He summoned all his courage and took a deep breath. He flapped his tiny wings and flew high into the sky. Pip felt like he was flying for the first time. He was nervous, but he knew he had to save his mother.

Pip finally reached the owl's nest, where his mother was held captive. The owl was huge and fierce, but Pip wasn't afraid anymore. He bravely flew towards the owl, and with all his might, he pecked the owl's eyes. The owl was blinded and released Pip's mother.

Pip and his mother flew back to their cozy nest, safe and sound. Pip was proud of himself. He never knew he had

such courage. From that day on, Pip was never afraid of flying again. He learned that sometimes we have to face our fears to protect those we love. Pip was a little bird with big courage, and his bravery saved the day.

~ The Lost Kitten ~

Once upon a time, in a cozy little village, a tiny kitten named Kiki was out playing with her siblings. They were having so much fun chasing each other's tails and playing hide and seek, that Kiki didn't realize she had wandered away from her family.

Suddenly, Kiki looked up and found herself all alone in a strange and unfamiliar place. The trees around her seemed to tower high into the sky, casting long shadows that made her feel scared and lonely.

But Kiki didn't give up. She bravely set out to explore her surroundings, even though every step made her tiny paws tremble with fear. She sniffed around, listening for any familiar sounds, but all she heard was the rustling of leaves and the distant hooting of an owl.

The night began to fall, and Kiki realized she was lost. She meowed for help, but no one came to her rescue. It was then that she decided to use her wits and find her way back home.

Kiki remembered that her mother always said to look for the North Star, and follow it to safety. With newfound courage, Kiki set out on her journey, keeping her eyes fixed on the brightest star in the sky.

After hours of walking, Kiki finally saw a faint light in the distance. It was the light from her family's cottage! She sprinted towards it, and soon enough, she was back in the arms of her loving mother.

From that day on, Kiki realized that even though the world can be a scary and unfamiliar place, she was strong and brave enough to face any challenge that came her way.

~ The Mighty Mouse ~

A Story About Courage

Once upon a time, in a cozy little mouse hole, lived a tiny mouse named Milo. He dreamed of being a hero, just like the ones he read about in books. But everyone knew that Milo was the smallest mouse in town, and he didn't have any muscles to speak of.

One day, while Milo was out foraging for food, he heard his friends crying for help. They were trapped in a dark corner by a mean old cat! Milo knew he had to do something, but he was scared.

Then, he remembered his dream of being a hero, and he decided to be brave. He scampered up to the top of the cat's back and started biting and scratching with all his might. The cat was so surprised that it started to thrash around, giving Milo's friends the chance to escape.

After a long and difficult fight, Milo emerged victorious,

covered in scratches and bruises. But his friends cheered for him, calling him "The Mighty Mouse" and thanking him for his bravery. From that day on, Milo knew that even the smallest among us can be heroes.

And so, whenever anyone needed help, Milo was always there, ready to show off his mighty muscles and his even mightier heart.

Letting Go and Focusing on What You Can Control

Stoics believe that letting go and focusing on what you can control helps you be happier and more peaceful. When you focus on things that are outside of your control, like the weather or what other people think of you, you'll just get frustrated and upset. But if you focus on things that you can control, like your own thoughts, feelings, and actions, you'll feel more in control and happier.

When you let go of things that are outside of your control, you're also less likely to be upset or disappointed. Maybe you wanted something really badly, but you didn't get it. If you let go and focus on what you can control, you'll be able to find other things that make you happy and feel fulfilled.

So let go of things that are outside of your control and focus on what you can control. You'll be happier, more peaceful, and ready for whatever comes your way.

~ The Stray in the Park ~

**A Story About Letting Go and
Focusing on What You Can Control**

Once upon a time, there was a kind-hearted boy who stumbled upon a stray dog in the park. He immediately fell in love with the furry creature and decided to take him home. He gave the dog a warm bed, delicious treats, and lots of love.

But one day, the boy received a call from the dog's owner. They had been searching for their beloved pet for weeks and were overjoyed to have found him. The boy was devastated at the thought of saying goodbye to his new furry friend, but he knew it was the right thing to do.

As the boy tearfully handed the dog back to his owner, he was comforted by the fact that he had done a good deed. He had taken care of the dog when he was in need and had helped him find his way back home. The boy understood that letting go of what we love can be difficult, but sometimes it's the most Stoic thing to do - accepting what is not in our control and focusing on what we can control.

In the end, the boy felt proud of himself for doing the right thing and for being a good friend to the dog. He knew that even though he couldn't keep the dog, he had made a positive impact on his life. The boy smiled, feeling grateful for the time they had spent together and knowing that he had done what was right.

~ Lila's Move ~

Once upon a time, there was a girl named Lila who had to move to a new town. She was sad because she wouldn't see her best friend, Zoé, anymore. She tried to convince her parents to stay, but they couldn't because of their jobs. Lila felt hopeless and upset.

When she arrived at her new house, she saw a girl outside with a skateboard. Her name was Raksha, and she asked Lila if she wanted to play. At first, Lila was nervous, but Raksha was kind and friendly, so they played together.

Lila thanked Raksha for being her new friend. She was excited to see what other fun things they could do together.

As time passed, Lila missed Zoé less and less. She didn't forget her old friend, but instead, she learned to cherish the happy memories they shared. Lila realized that holding on to the past was not helping her make new memories or appreciate the new opportunities life was offering her. She learned the stoic principle of letting go and focusing on what she could control, which helped her find happiness and contentment in her new life.

In the end, Lila understood that even though change can be hard, it can also be an opportunity for growth and new experiences. She learned to trust that life would always offer new opportunities, and that by focusing on what she could control, she could create positive outcomes even in the midst of challenging circumstances.

~ The School Project ~

Once upon a time, there were five friends named Amara,
Cyrus, Darian, Lyn, and Kaida. They were tasked with
creating a project on their favorite animal habitat. Amara
suggested the African savanna, but the others didn't
like the idea. Cyrus suggested the coral reef, and it was
ultimately chosen. Amara became sad and disappointed
that her idea wasn't picked.

She went back home and talked to her grandfather,
who asked her why she was sad. Amara explained the
situation, and her grandfather taught her about Stoic
values. He said, "You can't control what others choose,
but you can control your attitude towards it. You can be
sad and let it affect you, or you can focus on what you can
control and be proud of your effort."

Amara thought about her grandfather's words and decided
to focus on what she could control. She went back to the
group and continued to work on the project to the best
of her abilities. When they presented their project to the
class, it was met with a standing ovation. Everyone loved

their creative and unique take on the coral reef habitat, and Amara felt proud of her contribution to the project.

Her grandfather's Stoic lesson had taught her that letting go of things outside her control and focusing on what she could control could lead to unexpected successes. She learned that it wasn't about winning or losing, but about doing her best and being proud of her effort.

~ The Rainy Day ~

The sun was shining bright and the birds were singing in the sky. A group of friends decided to plan a picnic to enjoy the lovely weather. They packed their favorite snacks, blankets, and toys to have a fun-filled day in the park.

As they reached the park, the sky suddenly turned grey and a few drops of rain started to fall. The friends looked at each other in disbelief and started blaming each other for not checking the weather forecast. They became upset and frustrated, not knowing what to do.

But then, one friend had an idea. "Let's find a sheltered area and enjoy our picnic there!" he exclaimed. The friends loved the idea and immediately started searching for a spot. They found a cozy gazebo, covered with vines and flowers, where they could enjoy their snacks and drinks while listening to the pitter-patter of the rain.

After eating, the friends decided to have some fun in the rain. They splashed around in the puddles, danced to the rhythm of the rain, and had a great time together. They realized that they couldn't control the weather, but they could control their attitude towards it. They let go of their frustration and focused on what they could control, which led to a fun and memorable day.

~ The Lost Toy ~

Once upon a time, there was a girl named Olivia who had
a favorite toy. It was a pink unicorn plushie that she took
with her everywhere. One day, she went to the park with
her family and played with her unicorn. But as
they were leaving, she realized her
beloved toy was gone.

Olivia searched high and
low, under every bench
and behind every tree,
but couldn't find it. She
started to feel very sad
and began to cry.

Her mother saw how upset
she was and hugged her,
telling her gently that sometimes we lose things and
we can't control it. She suggested that they go home and
try to forget about the lost toy.

At first, Olivia didn't understand. How could she forget
her favorite toy? But as they walked back to the car, she

44

started to notice all the other toys she had at home. Her collection of stuffed animals, her dolls, and her board games. She realized that she had many things to enjoy and play with.

Olivia learned that it's important to enjoy the things we have while we have them. She still missed her unicorn, but she knew that she had other toys to play with and that she could create new memories with them.

~ Danny's Paper Boat Adventure ~

A Story About Letting Go and Focusing on What You Can Control

Danny and his dad had spent the whole afternoon creating a paper boat. It was a masterpiece, with colorful patterns and a sail made of tissue paper. Danny was so excited to see it float on the water, but as soon as they launched it, a strong gust of wind carried it away.

Danny tried to catch it with a stick, but it was too far from the shore. He started to get upset and frustrated, but his dad reminded him of the stoic lesson they had talked about before.

"Remember, Danny, we can't control the wind, but we can control our reaction to it," his dad said.

Danny took a deep breath and tried to let go of his attachment to the paper boat. He focused on what he could control and came up with a solution.

"Dad, let's create another paper boat, but this time, we'll

attach a string to it. That way, it won't get lost," Danny suggested.

His dad smiled and nodded. Together, they created a new paper boat and attached a string to it. They launched it again, and this time, it floated peacefully on the water.

As they walked back home, Danny realized that his dad's lesson about letting go and focusing on what they could control wasn't just about the boat. It was a lesson for life, about accepting things outside of their power and focusing on what they could control.

Self-Discipline

Self-discipline is like being the boss of your own actions and decisions. It means choosing to do things that are good for you, even if they're hard or you don't feel like doing them.

For example, let's say you have a big math test coming up, and you really want to play video games instead of studying. Self-discipline means saying to yourself, "I really want to play video games, but I know that studying for my test is more important. So I'm going to study first, and then play later as a reward for my hard work."

Stoics believe that being self-disciplined helps you achieve your goals and be successful. When you have self-discipline, you can make a plan, stick to it, and get things done. Self-discipline is good because it helps you achieve your goals and become a better person. When you have self-discipline, you can resist temptations that might lead you astray and focus on what's important. You'll also feel more proud of yourself when you accomplish something through your own hard work and determination.

When you're self-disciplined, you're also more in control of your emotions and your actions. Maybe you feel angry or upset, but if you have self-discipline, you can control those feelings and act in a way that's calm and respectful. This helps you be a better friend and make better choices.

So remember, being self-disciplined is like being the boss of yourself. It might not always be easy, but it will help you become a better person and achieve your goals in life.

~ The Chocolate Bar ~

A Story About Self-Discipline

Once upon a time, there was a child named Jeanne who loved chocolate more than anything. One day, she found a big, delicious-looking chocolate bar in the cupboard. She couldn't resist and ate the whole thing in one sitting! But soon after, she felt a sharp pain in her tummy.

Her parents came to check on her and saw what had happened. They sat down with Jeanne and explained the importance of self-discipline. They told her that eating too much candy at once could lead to an upset stomach and unhealthy habits.

Jeanne was sad that she didn't get to enjoy the chocolate bar properly, so her parents suggested that she try again, but with a different approach. They encouraged her to practice self-discipline and only have a small piece each day.

At first, it was hard for Jeanne to resist the temptation of the chocolate bar, but she remembered her parents' advice and managed to stick to just a small piece. And do you know what? Not only did she avoid getting a tummy ache, but she actually enjoyed the chocolate bar more!

From then on, Jeanne learned the importance of self-discipline and how it can lead to more enjoyable experiences. So remember, self-discipline may be tough, but it's worth it in the end!

~ The Great Garden Race ~

Once upon a time, in a small village, a group of children decided to have a friendly competition. They called it "The Great Garden Race." Each child would plant a small garden and see whose plants grew the best.

Lucy, Tommy, and Sam were very disciplined. They prepared the soil, carefully planted seeds, and created a schedule to water and weed their gardens. They worked diligently each day to ensure their gardens would flourish.

On the other side of the village, Max, Damo, and Leo were more carefree. They scattered their seeds haphazardly, watered their gardens whenever they remembered, and often ignored the weeds.

Weeks passed, and the children eagerly awaited the day of the big reveal. When the day finally arrived, they gathered around Lucy, Tommy, and Sam's gardens.

To their amazement, the gardens were filled with vibrant, colorful flowers and plump, juicy vegetables.

Next, they visited Max, Damo, and Leo's gardens. The sight was quite different! The plants were hidden beneath a jungle of weeds, and their flowers and vegetables looked sad and droopy.

It was clear who had won The Great Garden Race. The disciplined children enjoyed a delicious feast made from their garden's bounty, while the others learned an important lesson. They promised to practice self-discipline, so next year, their gardens would be just as beautiful and bountiful.

~ The Runaway Kite ~

In a bright, sunny town, there lived a young girl named Samira. For her birthday, she received the most beautiful kite she had ever seen. It was a dazzling rainbow of colors with a long, flowing tail.

Samira was so excited that she couldn't wait to fly her new kite. Instead of asking her father to teach her the proper techniques, she rushed to the park on a particularly windy day.

With a big grin on her face, Samira let her kite soar into the sky. At first, the kite danced gracefully, its tail fluttering behind like a ribbon. But soon, the wind picked up, and Samira began to struggle with controlling her runaway kite.

In a sudden gust, the kite was torn from her hands and carried away by the wind. Samira watched helplessly as it tangled itself in the branches of a tall tree. She felt sad and realized her lack of self-discipline had led to this predicament.

Determined to learn, Samira asked her father for help. He patiently showed her how to handle the kite and respond to the wind's whims. Samira practiced and grew more confident in her newfound skill.

With her self-discipline and perseverance, Samira returned to the park, ready to fly her kite once more. This time, she expertly guided it through the sky, delighting in the colorful display as it danced gracefully above her.

~ The Untidy Room ~

Once upon a time, there was a child named Silvio who had a really messy room. Toys were scattered everywhere, clothes were piled high, and books were mixed in with the mess. Silvio loved playing with all of his toys, but he often lost them in the clutter.

One day, Silvio's mom asked him to find his favorite toy car so they could play together. Silvio searched and searched, but he couldn't find it anywhere! He looked under piles of clothes, in between stacks of books, and even in the corners of his room.

Finally, Silvio realized that his messy room was the reason he couldn't find his toy. His mom explained the importance of self-discipline and keeping his space tidy. She told him that it's easier to find things and move around in a clean room.

Silvio decided to take on the challenge and clean up his room. It wasn't easy at first, but he started with small steps like putting away his toys after playing with them and folding his clothes neatly. As he worked, he noticed how much easier it was to find things and move around in his newly cleaned room.

From then on, Max made a habit of tidying up after himself and practicing self-discipline. Not only did it make his life easier and help him find his toys, but he also felt better living in a tidy room and enjoyed spending more time in his room. He could sit and read a book or play with his toys without feeling overwhelmed by the clutter. So remember, self-discipline isn't just about keeping things neat and tidy, it's also about feeling good about yourself!

~ Daisy the Dolphin's Swim Meet ~

A Story About Self-Discipline

In a dazzling bay, Daisy the Dolphin was known for her incredible swimming skills. She loved flipping and twirling, leaving a trail of sparkling water. However, she didn't enjoy practice.

With the swim meet approaching, Coach Clam encouraged Daisy to practice with self-discipline. "If you want to succeed, you need to practice consistently," he advised. But Daisy didn't listen. Daisy watched her favorite underwater TV show instead of practicing. She thought she could catch up later.

The swim meet arrived, and the bay buzzed with excitement. When it was Daisy's turn, her lack of practice soon showed. She struggled to keep up, her flips and twirls not as smooth as before.

Feeling disappointed, Daisy asked Coach Clam how to

improve her self-discipline. Coach Clam shared two helpful tips: "First, think about the long-term consequences of your actions. Imagine how great you'll be if you practice consistently, and how you might struggle if you don't. Second, find joy in everything you do. Make practice, learning, or even cleaning your room a fun game. When you enjoy the task, self-discipline comes naturally."

Daisy took Coach Clam's advice to heart. She began visualizing her long-term success and found creative ways to make practice enjoyable. As she flipped and twirled more gracefully than ever, Daisy became a shining example for her friends in the bay, proving that with self-discipline and a little fun, anything is possible.

Temperance

Temperance is a superpower that helps you control your feelings and stay calm and balanced! It's like having a magic potion that helps you stay in control of your emotions, even when things get tough.

Stoics believe that having temperance helps you be in control of your emotions and actions. When something happens that makes you feel angry, sad, or scared, temperance helps you take a deep breath and think before you act. It's like being a master of your own mind, and not letting your emotions take over.

Why is temperance good? Well, think about a time when you got really upset and said or did something you regretted later. Maybe you got into a fight with a friend or said something mean to a sibling. When you have temperance, you can avoid those kinds of situations and keep your relationships strong.

Temperance also helps you make good choices and stay on the right path. It's like having a compass that points you in the right direction, even when there are obstacles in your way.

So remember, use your temperance to add just the right amount of emotions to your life! You'll be in control of your feelings and actions, and you'll be able to handle any situation with grace and calmness.

~ The Big Soccer Match ~

Once upon a time, in a small town, there was a talented soccer player named Maria. She was swift and strong, but her emotions often got the best of her. During games, Maria would get frustrated and angry, earning penalties and upsetting her teammates.

One sunny day, her coach pulled her aside and introduced her to the idea of temperance. He explained the importance of remaining calm and focused on the field. Maria listened carefully and promised to practice emotional control.

Over the next few weeks, Maria learned to take deep breaths and count to ten when she felt her emotions bubbling up. She noticed that the more she practiced, the easier it became to stay composed during games.

Finally, the day of the big soccer match arrived. The air was electric with excitement. Maria's team was playing their biggest rival, and the championship was on the line. As the game started, Maria took a deep breath and reminded herself to stay calm.

In the final minutes of the match, the score was tied. Maria saw an opportunity to score the winning goal. Instead of giving in to anxiety, she took a deep breath, focused, and kicked the ball with all her might. The ball soared through the air and landed in the back of the net!

Her teammates erupted in cheers, and everyone rushed to hug Maria. Her newfound emotional control had not only helped her perform better but also won the championship for her team. From that day on, Maria was a shining example of temperance and a true soccer star.

~ The Angry Bird ~

A Story About Temperance

Once upon a time, there was an angry bird named Alex. Alex had a habit of losing his temper over little things, like when the worms were too wriggly or when the tree branch was too wobbly. His anger would take over, and he would start pecking at things and knocking them down.

One day, Alex's anger got the best of him. He was so mad that he flew into a birdhouse and broke it. Alex hurt himself in the process and had to sit on a branch, nursing his wounds.

As he sat there, Alex realized that his temper was causing him more harm than good. He decided to take a deep breath and try to control his emotions. Whenever he felt angry, he would count to ten and think about the consequences of his actions.

Slowly but surely, Alex began to see a change in his behavior. He stopped pecking at things and started to fly away when he felt his anger rising. The other birds noticed the change in Alex and started to invite him to their gatherings.

Soon enough, Alex became a happier bird. He no longer got angry over little things and enjoyed spending time with his bird friends. From then on, Alex learned that controlling his temper was the key to a happier life.

~ The Happy Hiker ~

Once upon a time, there was a young girl named Emily who loved to explore nature. One sunny day, she and her family set out on a hike through the forest. Emily was so excited to be outside in the fresh air and sunshine that she began to skip and hop down the trail.

As they climbed higher up the mountain, Emily's excitement only grew. She admired the trees, the birds, and the views of the valley below. But then, as she was skipping along, she didn't notice a big rock in her path. She tripped and tumbled down the trail.

Emily's parents rushed over to check on her and make sure she was okay. She had a few scrapes and bruises, but nothing too serious. After they helped her back up and dusted her off, her parents reminded her to be more careful and watch her step.

Emily realized that her excitement had made her forget to pay attention to where she was going. She slowed down and walked more carefully the rest of the way up the mountain, enjoying the sights but also being mindful of her surroundings.

As they reached the top of the mountain, Emily felt a great sense of accomplishment. She was proud of herself for being more careful and for making it to the summit. From then on, Emily learned to balance her enthusiasm with awareness, and she had many more safe and happy hikes with her family.

~ The Tale of Paul's Tantrum ~

Once upon a time, there was a little boy named Paul who had a big problem. Whenever things didn't go his way, he would throw a tantrum, stomping his feet and yelling as loud as he could.

One sunny day, Paul was playing with his friends at school. They decided to have a race during recess. Paul was sure he would win, but he tripped on a shoelace and came in last. He was furious!

His face turned red as a cherry, and he started to shout and cry. His friends were scared by his outburst and didn't want to play with him anymore. Paul felt sad and lonely.

Seeing this, his kind teacher Ms. Willow took him aside and whispered the secret of temperance. She told him to take deep breaths and count to ten whenever he felt upset. Paul promised to try.

The next day, the children raced again. Paul ran his fastest, but still didn't win. This time, he remembered Ms. Willow's advice. He took a deep breath, counted to ten, and managed to stay calm. He even congratulated the winner with a genuine smile.

To his surprise, his friends gathered around and cheered him on, saying, "Great job, Paul! You kept your cool!" Paul beamed with happiness, grateful for the lesson in emotional control that brought his friends back. And from that day on, Paul embraced the stoic value of temperance, knowing it would help him become a better friend and a happier person.

~ The Raging River ~

Edwige and Sarah were excited to go on a rafting trip down the river. As they were navigating the river, they encountered a rough patch of water that was causing their raft to sway uncontrollably. Edwige, who tended to let her emotions get the best of her, began to panic and scream, making the situation worse.

Thankfully, Sarah, with a calm and collected demeanor, took control of the situation. "Edwige, take deep breaths and try to stay calm. We can do this, but we need to work together," she said, guiding Edwige to paddle in sync with her to avoid the dangerous rocks and currents.

Despite the rough waters, they were able to navigate the raft safely to the end of their journey.

As they celebrated their success, Edwige apologized for her initial outburst and promised to work on her emotional control. "I'll try to remember to stay calm like you did, Sarah," she said, admiring Sarah's temperance under pressure. From that day on, Edwige made a conscious effort to work on her emotional control and become more like Sarah, who showed great temperance in the face of danger.

The friends learned that staying calm and collected in stressful situations can lead to better outcomes and stronger relationships. They all agreed that they couldn't have made it through the rough patch of water without Sarah's emotional control and level-headedness.

~ The Hot-Headed Fox ~

Once upon a time, in a forest filled with furry creatures, there was a hot-headed fox named Foxy. Whenever something didn't go his way, he would get so angry that his fur would stand on end and his eyes would glow red like hot coals. He would lash out, say hurtful things, and sometimes even break things.

One day, an old and wise fox approached Foxy and said, "My dear young friend, extreme emotions are like an inner monster that takes control of you. We all have that monster in ourselves, but if we don't tame that monster, we will let it control us and destroy our lives."

Foxy didn't quite understand what the old fox meant. But the wise fox continued, "When you feel yourself getting angry, take a deep breath and count to ten. Think about what you want to say and how you want to react. That's what we call temperance, my young friend."

Foxy took the wise fox's advice to heart and started to practice temperance. Whenever he felt himself getting angry, he would take a deep breath and count to ten. He started to communicate his feelings in a calmer way, and as a result, he built stronger relationships with those around him.

And so, Foxy learned the stoic principle of temperance and tamed his inner monster. He became a happier and more peaceful fox, and everyone in the forest lived happily ever after.

⋮ Sobriety and Seeking Joy in Simplicity ⋮

Explanation

Sobriety is like being content with what you have and not always wanting more. Imagine you're at a party, and there are lots of toys and treats and games. You might want all of them, but if you keep wanting more and more, you'll never be satisfied. Sobriety is like being happy with what you already have and not always needing more.

Stoics believe that being sober and seeking joy in simplicity helps you be happier and more content. When you learn to be happy with simple things like playing outside or spending time with your family, you realize that happiness doesn't come from things. It comes from inside of you.

When you're sober, you're also less likely to be upset or disappointed. If you don't need fancy things to be happy, you won't be sad if you can't get them. You'll be able to enjoy the simple things in life and be happy with them.

So be content with what you have and find joy in the simple things in life! You'll be happier, more content, and a great example to others.

~ The True Meaning of Happiness ~

A Story About Sobriety and Seeking Joy in Simplicity

Once upon a time, there was a boy named Liam who had every toy he could ever want. But despite having so many toys, he still felt bored and unfulfilled. He would always beg his parents for more toys and never seemed to be happy with what he had.

One day, while playing in the park, Liam met a boy named Noah who was happily playing with rocks and sticks. Liam couldn't understand why anyone would play with rocks and sticks when they could have cool toys like he did.

But Noah said something that stuck with Liam. "I don't need toys to be happy," Noah said. "I can be happy with little or nothing."

Liam thought about what Noah had said. "Maybe Noah's right," he thought. "I do have a lot of toys, but I'm still not happy. And there's always something new that I want."

That night, Liam looked around his room and realized that he had so many toys that he didn't even play with. He felt guilty for always wanting more when there were other kids who didn't have any toys. The next day, Liam decided to donate most of his toys to children who didn't have any toys. His mom and dad were surprised, but they were proud of Liam for being so generous.

"Wow, Liam," said his mom. "That's very kind of you! You know, it's true what they say. The best things in life aren't things."

From that day on, Liam realized that he didn't need toys to be happy. He enjoyed spending time with his friends and family, playing games, and exploring the outdoors. He learned that true happiness comes from the simple things in life.

~ The Magic of the Starry Night ~

Once upon a time, in a bustling city filled with shimmering lights, lived a young girl named Millie. She was always surrounded by the hum of technology and the bright glow of screens. The stars in the night sky were hidden behind the city's constant buzz.

One summer, Millie was sent to visit her grandparents in the peaceful countryside. At first, she felt bored and missed the city's excitement. One night, her grandfather decided to show her something magical. He took her hand and led her up a gentle hill, away from the cozy house.

As they reached the top, Millie gasped in amazement. Above them, the night sky was a velvety blanket, sprinkled with twinkling stars. Her grandfather pointed out constellations and shared ancient stories about brave heroes, mythical creatures, and faraway worlds.

Millie listened, captivated by the simple beauty of the stars and the enchanting tales they held. The city lights no longer seemed as exciting as the vast, mysterious

78

universe above. Her heart swelled with joy and wonder as she lay on the soft grass, gazing at the sparkling sky.

From that magical night, Millie learned to cherish the beauty of simplicity and find joy in the natural world. Whenever she looked up at the stars, she would remember her grandfather's wise words and the enchanting stories that danced among the celestial wonders.

~ The Little Wooden Boat ~

A Story About Sobriety and Seeking Joy in Simplicity

Once upon a time, in a quaint seaside town, lived a curious girl named Maddy. She often strolled by the marina, admiring the luxurious boats that sparkled in the sun. She dreamed of one day owning such a fancy vessel herself.

One birthday, her loving grandfather gifted her a small, simple wooden boat he had crafted with his own hands. At first, Maddy felt a twinge of disappointment, but she soon decided to give the little boat a chance.

Maddy and her little wooden boat ventured out onto a calm lake, gliding peacefully over the shimmering water. With each adventure, Maddy grew fonder of her humble vessel. She learned to appreciate the gentle lapping of waves, the soft breeze, and the chorus of birdsong.

One sunny afternoon, as Maddy sat by the lake, she realized that true happiness could be found in the simplest of things. Her little wooden boat had shown her that the most precious moments in life come not from material possessions, but from the experiences and memories we create.

Embracing the Stoic principles of finding joy in simplicity and being content with what she had, Maddy cherished her little wooden boat and the valuable lessons it had taught her. She no longer yearned for a fancy boat, for she knew that the greatest treasures in life lie not in possessions, but in the heart.

~ The Humble Tea Party ~

Once upon a sunny day, Timmy, a lively little boy, decided to throw the most extravagant tea party ever. He spent weeks planning, using his allowance to buy the fanciest decorations and tastiest treats he could find. He wanted his tea party to be the talk of the town!

On the day of the party, dark clouds rolled in, and a storm knocked out the power. Timmy felt his heart sink as his elaborate plans crumbled. His wise grandfather saw the disappointment on Timmy's face and suggested a new plan: a humble, candlelit tea party with homemade treats and games.

Timmy hesitated but agreed to give it a try. As the guests arrived, they gathered around the flickering candles and shared warm, delicious cookies. The children played simple games, laughing and enjoying each other's company.

To Timmy's surprise, the cozy atmosphere made the party even better! Everyone felt special and appreciated, and the laughter echoed through the room. Timmy realized that the true joy of a tea party wasn't in the fancy decorations or expensive treats, but in the connections made with friends and the fun they shared.

From that day on, Timmy embraced the beauty of simplicity and the power of friendship. He discovered that the most memorable moments are often found in the humblest of gatherings, where laughter, love, and happiness shine brighter than any extravagance.

~ The Witch's Deceitful Wishes ~

Once upon a time, there was a little girl named Kaori. She was a happy child, but always dreamed of having more. One day, while playing in the forest, she met an old witch who offered to grant her as many wishes as she wanted.

Kaori was ecstatic! She wished for a new bike, a puppy, and a big house with a swimming pool. Each wish was granted, but the new things brought more problems than joy. The bike was too big and hard to ride, the puppy chewed up all her toys, and the big house made her feel lonely.

One day, Kaori met a wise old owl who explained the witch's evil plan. The witch wanted to make children unhappy by making them want more and more. But the best way to defeat the witch's plan was to learn to be happy with little.

Kaori realized that she already had everything she needed to be happy. She had her family, friends, and a cozy little house. She decided to stop making wishes for more and instead be grateful for what she had.

The witch never bothered Kaori again, and she lived happily ever after. From that day on, she knew that the secret to happiness was not in having more, but in being content with what she had.

Morality

Explanation

Morality is like being a superhero! Just like how superheroes save the day, being moral means doing the right thing even when no one is watching. It's about making choices that are good and fair, even if they're hard.

Let's say you're playing a game with your friends, and you could easily cheat to win. But, being moral means you would never cheat because it's not fair to the others playing. It's like having a special power that lets you make good choices!

Stoics believe that being moral means doing what's good, even if it's hard or nobody is looking. It's like being honest when you know you did something wrong, or helping a friend even when you don't want to. Being moral makes you feel proud of yourself, and other people will trust and respect you more.

But being moral isn't just about doing the right thing. It's also about thinking the right way. For example, if someone is mean to you, instead of wanting to hurt them back, being moral means trying to understand why they acted that way and trying to forgive them.

Being moral isn't always easy, but it's worth it. It helps you become a better person, make good choices, and live a happier life. And when we all follow the rules of morality, we can create a world where everyone can be safe, happy, and respected.

~ The Stolen Candy ~

Once upon a time, there was a little girl named Aanya who loved candy. Whenever she walked past a candy store, her eyes would light up with excitement. One day, she went into the candy store and saw a delicious-looking lollipop.

Her mouth watered, but she didn't have any money to buy it. She thought to herself, "No one would notice if I just take one."

Aanya slipped the lollipop into her pocket and started to walk out of the store. Suddenly, her conscience spoke up, "Aanya, that's not right. You should put the candy back and tell the store owner what you did." Aanya knew her conscience was right, so she went back into the store and put the lollipop on the counter. She told the store owner what she had almost done and apologized.

The store owner was impressed by Aanya's honesty and

thanked her for being truthful. As a reward, he gave her the lollipop for free! Aanya felt a warm and fuzzy feeling in her heart, knowing that doing the right thing had brought her more joy than the candy ever could have.

Overwhelmed with joy, Aanya skipped out of the store with her lollipop in hand. As she walked down the street, she noticed a little boy. Without a second thought, Aanya ran up to him and offered him the lollipop. Aanya felt happy to share her good fortune with someone else.

From that day on, Aanya made it a habit to look for opportunities to help others and do good deeds. She realized that no candy or material possession could bring her the same sense of fulfillment as being kind and honest, no matter how tempting the candy may be.

~ The Selfless Dove ~ and the Selfish Crow

Once upon a time, in a lush garden full of bright flowers and sweet fruits, lived a gentle dove and a cunning crow. The garden was a paradise for all the creatures who lived there.

The dove was kind-hearted and always thought of others, while the crow was selfish and only cared about itself. The animals in the garden admired the dove's generosity and felt wary of the crow's antics.

One day, the skies turned gray, and a terrible drought befell the garden. The once-abundant food and water became scarce. The crow, thinking only of itself, began to hoard all the remaining resources, leaving the other animals to suffer.

The selfless dove, despite its own needs, shared what little it had with the other animals. The dove's actions sparked a wave of kindness, and soon, many animals started to help one another, following the dove's example.

As the drought continued, the crow's selfishness left it all alone, while the dove's selflessness brought the animals closer together. The garden's inhabitants worked as a team, supporting each other through the hard times.

Eventually, the rains returned, and the garden flourished once more. The animals never forgot the dove's kindness, and they learned an important lesson about the Stoic principle of morality: being selfless and caring for others, even in times of adversity, brings happiness and harmony to all.

And so, the dove remained a beloved member of the garden community, while the selfish crow was left to ponder the consequences of its actions.

~ The Cheating Contestant ~

Once upon a time, there was a school contest where the winner would receive a grand prize. A boy named Ben was determined to win, no matter what. He thought about cheating and even made a plan to do so. But, little did he know, his plan was going to fail.

When the contest began, Ben tried to cheat, but his plan was discovered, and he was disqualified. Ben was disappointed, but what hurt him the most was that his friends lost respect for him. They were upset that he had even thought about cheating, and they didn't want to be friends with someone who wasn't honest.

Ben learned a valuable lesson that day. He realized that cheating was not worth it and that there were negative consequences to his actions. He knew that he had let his friends down, and he felt terrible about it.

From then on, Ben decided to always be honest, even if it meant losing. He learned that there is no morality in cheating, and it can hurt others and oneself. He started to rebuild his relationships with his friends, and he became known for his honesty and integrity.

Ben learned a valuable lesson about morality - cheating may seem like an easy way to win, but it ultimately leads to negative consequences. It's always better to do the right thing, even when it's hard, because honesty and integrity are what truly matter.

~ The Bully ~

Once upon a time, there was a boy named Tim who loved to pick on his classmates. He thought it was funny to tease them and make them feel small, but he never realized how much it hurt their feelings. That is until a group of older kids began to bully him too. Suddenly, Tim understood how painful it was to be on the receiving end of such harsh words and actions.

Tim felt remorseful for his behavior, and he decided to make amends. The next day, he apologized to all the kids he had hurt, and he promised to never bully anyone again. But that wasn't enough for him. He wanted to do more to help others and prevent bullying from happening in the future.

So, Tim started an anti-bullying campaign at school. He made posters with positive messages and hosted a school-wide assembly to talk about the importance of kindness and respect. Slowly but surely, the school culture began to shift, and more students started to treat each other with empathy and understanding.

Tim realized that his past actions had negative consequences, but he also saw how his decision to change and become more moral had positive consequences. He learned that being kind and respectful to others was not only the right thing to do, but it also made him feel better about himself. And that's the stoic principle of morality - doing the right thing even when it's hard, because it's the right thing to do.

Humility

Humility is when we don't think we're better than others, even if we're really good at something. Imagine you're playing a game with your friends, and you're really good at it. Instead of bragging and showing off, humility means saying something like, "We all did a great job together!"

Humility is good because it helps us be kind and fair to others. When we're humble, we listen to others and learn from them. We don't put them down or think we're better than them. This makes people like us more and want to be our friends.

Being humble also helps us avoid being too proud and making mistakes. Sometimes, when we think we're the best, we stop learning and trying new things. We might even be mean to others or think we're always right. Humility reminds us that we still have things to learn and that it's okay to make mistakes.

Humility is also about admitting when we make mistakes and being happy that we can still improve. So, let's remember to be humble, even when we mess up. We can say sorry, try again, and learn from our mistakes. And that's a great thing because it means we're growing and getting better every day!

~ The Clever Fox Who Learned to Be Quiet ~

Once upon a time, in a forest filled with tall trees and wildflowers, there lived a young and clever fox named Franny. Franny was the smartest fox in all the land, and she loved to tell everyone about it. She would often boast about her intelligence and how she could solve any problem that came her way.

At first, Franny's friends and family were impressed with her smarts. But as time went on, they grew tired of hearing about it. They found her boasting to be annoying and even started to avoid her company.

One day, Franny's parents noticed her behavior and decided to have a talk with her. They told her that it was great to be smart, but that it was important to develop other skills too, like humility and kindness. They explained that when you're good at something, you don't have to tell everyone about it. It's better to say nothing and let people naturally find out your quality.

Franny realized that her parents were right. She decided to stop boasting and started to focus on being humble and kind to others. As she did, she noticed that her friends and family started to enjoy her company again. They even started to notice her intelligence on their own, without her having to say a word.

From that day on, Franny learned that true intelligence comes from more than just being smart. It comes from being kind, humble, and letting your qualities shine on their own.

~ The Boastful Squirrel ~

Once upon a time, in a lush forest, there was a proud squirrel named Chestnut. Chestnut believed that it was the best squirrel in the forest, boasting about its agility, intelligence, and quick reflexes to its fellow squirrels. It never asked for help and always worked alone.

One day, while gathering nuts for the winter, Chestnut came across a massive acorn. Overconfident in its abilities, Chestnut decided to carry the acorn by itself. However, the acorn was much heavier than Chestnut anticipated, and it struggled to carry it.

As Chestnut was carrying the acorn, it slipped from its grasp and fell to the ground, cracking open. The other squirrels in the forest saw what had happened and offered to help, but Chestnut refused their assistance.

Determined to prove its superiority, Chestnut spent the rest of the day trying to gather as many nuts as possible on its own. Meanwhile, the other squirrels worked together and collected far more nuts than Chestnut.

At the end of the day, Chestnut returned to its nest with only a handful of nuts, feeling exhausted and embarrassed. Chestnut realized that it was not the best squirrel in the forest and that it needed the help of its fellow squirrels to survive.

From that day on, Chestnut became more humble and learned to appreciate the value of teamwork.

~ The Mysterious Helper ~

Once upon a time, in a bustling school, mysterious good deeds were happening when no one was looking. Someone was cleaning up messes, fixing posters, and doing other nice things for the school. The students and teachers were amazed and grateful, but no one knew who was behind it all.

One day, two brothers, Omar and Ali, came home from school. Omar excitedly told their father about the good deeds, but Ali remained silent and avoided eye contact. The father noticed Ali's strange behavior and asked to speak to him alone.

"Do you know who was behind the good deeds at your school?" the father asked Ali, hoping for an honest answer. After a moment of hesitation, Ali finally admitted, "It was me."

"Why didn't you tell anyone?" the father asked.

102

"I didn't need to," Ali replied. "I'm just happy to help."

The father smiled and explained that what Ali was showing was called humility, a wonderful quality that not everyone possesses. He told Ali how proud he was of him and how important it is to do good things without expecting recognition.

From that day on, Ali continued to do good deeds for his school, happy just to know he was making a difference. He learned a valuable lesson about humility and the power of doing good deeds without seeking recognition.

~ The Arrogant Ant ~ and the Helpful Bee

Once upon a time in a bustling garden, there lived an arrogant ant named Andy. He was known throughout the garden for boasting about his strength and intelligence. Andy believed that he was the best and the smartest insect of all, and he didn't need anyone's help.

One day, Andy decided to build the grandest ant colony the garden had ever seen. As he started to work, a humble bee named Betty buzzed by. She saw Andy struggling to lift a tiny pebble and offered to help.

"No, thank you!" Andy huffed. "I can do it all by myself."

Betty quietly flew away, leaving Andy to his task. As the days passed, Andy grew more and more tired, and his progress was slow. He realized he couldn't build the grand colony alone.

One morning, Betty returned and, without saying a word, began helping Andy. Together, they worked tirelessly, and soon, the grandest ant colony was complete. Its tunnels were intricate, and the chambers were spacious, filled with the happy buzz of fellow ants.

Andy felt a warmth in his heart as he looked at what they had accomplished. He had learned the importance of humility and the value of teamwork. From that day on, Andy became a kinder, more helpful ant, always ready to lend a hand or a wing to a friend in need.

Empathy

Empathy is when you try to understand how someone else is feeling. For example, if your friend falls down and hurts themselves, you might feel sorry for them and want to help them, instead of laughing or making fun of them. That's what empathy is all about - trying to imagine how others are feeling and being kind to them, even when things aren't going well.

Empathy is a good thing because it helps us be kind to others. When we understand how someone is feeling, we can help them feel better. For example, if your friend is feeling sad, you might tell them a joke or give them a hug to make them feel better.

Stoics believe that empathy is important because it helps us be better people. By understanding how others are feeling, we can be more patient and understanding with them. We can also learn from their experiences and become wiser ourselves.

Empathy is like a superpower that everyone can use. By trying to understand how others are feeling, we can make the world a better place. So, next time you see someone who looks sad or upset, try to imagine how they are feeling and think of ways to make them feel better.

~ Ruby's Change of Heart ~

Once upon a time, there was a little girl named Ava. She loved playing with her dolls and pretending she was a princess in a magical kingdom. But Ava was different from other children because she used a wheelchair to get around.

One day, Ava went to the park and saw a group of girls playing. She felt excited and asked if she could join in. But the other girls looked at her wheelchair and said, "No, sorry. We don't want to play with someone who can't run and jump like us."

Ava felt sad and alone. She didn't understand why they wouldn't play with her just because she was in a wheelchair. She watched the girls play from a distance, feeling left out.

One of the girls, named Ruby, felt bad about what had happened. She didn't like the way her friends were treating Ava. She argued with the other girls, saying that it wasn't fair to exclude someone just because they were different.

Finally, Ruby decided to go play with Ava instead. They played with dolls, had a tea party, and talked about their favorite princesses. Ruby realized that Ava had so much friendship to give and that being in a wheelchair didn't make her any less fun to play with.

From that day on, Ruby and Ava became good friends. Ruby learned that empathy was important, and that being kind to others can lead to strong friendships. And Ava learned that she was loved and accepted just the way she was, wheelchair and all.

~ The Ice Witch's Cold Heart ~

Once upon a time, in a magical kingdom covered in glistening snow, the Ice Witch ruled with a heart as cold as ice. No one dared to approach her, for she would freeze them with her icy breath.

One sunny day, a young girl named Zaya ventured into the kingdom. Zaya had a heart full of warmth and

kindness that could melt the ice around her. As she walked, flowers bloomed, and icicles dripped like tiny waterfalls.

Bravely, Zaya approached the Ice Witch's palace. The Ice Witch glared down at her, preparing to

110

freeze Zaya just like the others. But Zaya simply smiled, her big brown eyes sparkling with empathy.

"Your Majesty," Zaya said gently, "I can see that you're lonely. But if you let love and empathy into your heart, you'll find friends in this snowy kingdom."

The Ice Witch scoffed, but something in Zaya's words touched her cold heart. She hesitated, and at that moment, a tiny crack formed in the ice around her heart.

Zaya continued to visit the Ice Witch, sharing stories, laughter, and empathy. Slowly but surely, the ice around the Witch's heart melted away, revealing a heart full of love and kindness.

From that day on, the Ice Witch ruled with empathy, and the magical kingdom flourished, warmed by the newfound love and friendship between the Witch and her people. And everyone lived happily ever after.

~ The Lonely Bee ~ and the Caring Ants

Once upon a time, in a colorful meadow filled with buzzing bees and busy ants, there lived a lonely bee named Beebop. Beebop never showed empathy and was often rude to the other insects, making him quite unpopular.

One warm summer day, Beebop found himself lost and separated from his hive. Tired and hungry, he stumbled upon a colony of ants working together to carry food back to their nest.

Beebop watched the ants, feeling a pang of envy for their teamwork and camaraderie. Despite knowing about Beebop's indifference, the kind-hearted ants decided to help him.

The ants' leader, Amelia, approached Beebop and said,

"We know you've been unkind to others, but we believe everyone deserves empathy and kindness. Let us help you find your way home."

Touched by the ants' compassion, Beebop felt his heart swell with gratitude. With the ants' guidance, he soon found his way back to his hive.

From that day on, Beebop learned the importance of empathy and treated other insects with kindness and respect. The once lonely bee formed many new friendships, and the meadow became a happier, more harmonious place, buzzing with love and understanding.

~ The Grumpy Elephant ~ and the Tiny Mouse

A Story About Empathy

In a lush jungle filled with animals big and small, there lived a grumpy elephant named Mobby. Mobby was always grumbling, never showing empathy to his fellow creatures. He preferred to be left alone.

One sunny afternoon, a tiny mouse named Mimi found herself trapped in a hole, unable to climb out. Desperate, she cried for help, and her tiny voice reached Mobby's giant ears. Mobby heard Mimi's pleas but chose to ignore them. Mimi, with great struggle, managed to free herself alone.

Not long after, Mobby found himself in a tricky situation. While reaching for some leaves, his trunk became tangled in a tree's branches. Embarrassed, he tried to free himself but only managed to get more tangled.

Just then, Mimi scampered by and saw Mobby's predicament. She remembered how he ignored her, but she still gathered her mouse friends, and together they nibbled at the branches, freeing Mobby's trunk.

Surprised, Mobby asked Mimi, "Why did you help me when I didn't help you before?"

Mimi smiled and replied, "Because I believe in helping others no matter what."

Mobby understood the importance of empathy and felt his heart change. From that day on, he became a more considerate friend, and the jungle was filled with the laughter and joy of all the animals, big and small, living in harmony.

Gratitude

Gratitude is like having a magic power that helps you see all the good things in your life. Imagine you woke up one day, and all your toys were gone, and your house was just an empty room. You'd probably feel really sad and miss all the things you used to have. Gratitude is the opposite of that. It's when you look around and see all the things you have and feel happy and thankful for them.

Stoics believe that being grateful helps you be happier and more content. When you focus on what you have instead of what you don't have, you realize how many amazing things you already have in your life. Maybe you have a family who loves you, a pet who cuddles with you, or a favorite food that always makes you smile. When you're grateful for these things, you feel happier and more satisfied with your life.

Being grateful also helps you be kinder to others. When you realize how lucky you are, you want to share that luck with other people. Maybe you share your toys with a friend who doesn't have as many, or you help someone who needs it.

So be like a magician and use your gratitude power to see all the good things in your life and share that goodness with others!

~ The Parallel World ~ of Ungrateful Elvin

Once upon a time, in a colorful forest, there lived a young elf named Elvin. He was always grumbling, never happy with his work, food, or friends. Nothing seemed good enough for him.

One sunny day, an old, wise elf named Tylord overheard Elvin's endless complaints. Feeling a sense of responsibility, Tylord decided to teach the young elf the value of gratitude. He waved his magical staff and created a shimmering portal to a parallel world where Elvin had everything he thought he desired.

Elvin was amazed by the new world, but as time passed, he felt a strange emptiness. The fancy food tasted bland, the grand treehouse felt cold, and his new friends were not as kind as those he had left behind. He missed the laughter, the simple joys, and the warmth of his old life.

Seeing Elvin's sadness, wise Tylord appeared and asked, "Do you now understand the power of gratitude, Elvin?" With a heavy heart, Elvin nodded. "I do, wise Tylord. I took my life for granted, and now I see how truly blessed I was."

Tylord smiled gently and waved his staff once more, transporting Elvin back to his original world. Reunited with his friends and the familiar surroundings, Elvin felt a surge of gratitude. He vowed to appreciate every moment, every meal, and every friend from that day forward.

And so, Elvin the young elf learned the magic of gratitude and lived happily ever after.

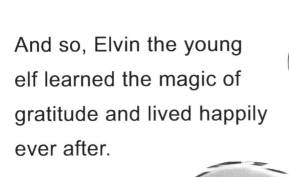

~ The Disappearing Toys ~

Once there was a boy named Antonio, who had a room full of toys. He had toy cars, dolls, building blocks, board games, puzzles, and more. His parents worked hard to give him everything he wanted, but Antonio never seemed to appreciate his toys. He would play with them for a little while, then leave them scattered all over the floor.

Antonio's parents tried to talk to him about the importance of being grateful, but he didn't understand. He thought that having lots of toys was just normal, and he didn't realize how lucky he was. He would always ask for more toys, never satisfied with what he already had.

One day, Antonio woke up to find that all of his toys were gone! He looked everywhere, but they had vanished into thin air. His parents explained to him that his toys were gone because he didn't appreciate them enough. At first, Antonio felt angry and confused. He couldn't understand why his toys had disappeared. But then, as he looked around his empty room, he started to realize just how much he had taken his toys for granted. He felt a deep sense of loss and wished that he could have them back.

The next day, when Antonio woke up, he found that his toys had magically reappeared! He felt so grateful to have them back that he hugged every single toy. From that day on, Antonio played with his toys every chance he got, and he made sure to appreciate them and take care of them.

Antonio learned that being grateful for what he had made him happier and more appreciative of the good things in his life. And who knows, maybe his toys even felt happier and more loved now that Antonio appreciated them more!

~ The Thankful Caterpillar ~

Once upon a time, in a garden filled with colorful flowers, there lived a little caterpillar named Carl. Carl was always wishing he could be something else, like a bird or a butterfly. He didn't appreciate his own unique qualities.

One day, Carl met a wise old butterfly who could see the caterpillar's struggles. The butterfly sat down next to Carl and asked him what was wrong.

"I just wish I could be something else, something better," Carl said.

The butterfly smiled and said, "But Carl, you are already something amazing. You are a caterpillar, and you have the power to transform into a beautiful butterfly."

Carl looked at the butterfly with surprise. "Really? I didn't know that," he said.

The butterfly nodded. "It's true, Carl. And you have so much to be thankful for. You have your health, your family, and the beauty of this garden."

Carl looked around at the flowers and the sunshine, and he felt a warm feeling in his heart. He realized he had been taking his life for granted.

"Thank you for reminding me," Carl said to the butterfly. "I'm grateful for everything I have."

And with those words, Carl felt a wave of happiness wash over him. He realized that he was already something special, and he didn't need to be anything else.

~ The Day the Lights Went Out ~

A Story About Gratitude

Once upon a time, there was a little girl named Adelaide. Adelaide was always amazed by everything around her, from the glittering stars in the sky to the blooming flowers in her backyard. She was grateful for every little thing in her life, but her parents didn't seem to share her enthusiasm.

One day, a big storm knocked out the power in their home. The parents were grumbling about the inconvenience and how they couldn't watch their favorite TV shows, but Adelaide was excited. She told her parents that they should be grateful for the experience because they could learn to appreciate the comforts of home that they usually took for granted.

As the day went on, the family played games by candlelight and told silly stories. Adelaide's parents began to see things through her grateful eyes and realized that they were grateful for the love and laughter they shared as a family, regardless of the lack of electricity.

But then, Adelaide surprised them all. She said, "We can also be thankful for the lack of comfort, because we have each other as a family, and that's all the comfort we really need!" Her parents looked at each other and smiled, realizing that their little girl was wise beyond her years.

From that day on, the family started expressing gratitude for all the little things in their lives, including each other. And Adelaide's parents learned that sometimes, the smallest and simplest things can bring the most joy and comfort.

Made in the USA
Las Vegas, NV
14 November 2024

11788415R00070